BELMONT !

MW00714849

Kingston Poets' Gallery

BELMONT HOUSE

Kingston Poets' Gallery

❧

Compiled and edited by
Elizabeth Greene

ARTFUL CODGER PRESS   2006

© Elizabeth Greene 2006
Printed in Canada
ISBN 0-9736161-7-2

Individual authors retain copyright for their own works in this publication.

LIBRARY AND ARCHIVES CANADA CATALOGUING IN PUBLICATION

Kingston poets' gallery / compiled and edited by Elizabeth Greene.
ISBN 0-9736161-7-2
1.Canadian poetry (English) – Ontario – Kingston. 2.Canadian poetry (English) – 21st century. I. Greene, Elizabeth, 1943-

PS8295.7.K56K56 2006 C811'.6080971372 C2006-901696-8

ARTFUL CODGER PRESS
10 GORDON STREET, KINGSTON, ONTARIO K7M3R9

CONTENTS

INTRODUCTION

A cold snowy January afternoon already darkening in the first days of 2005. I stumble into the Gallery Café, shake the snow layers from my head and coat, look appreciatively at Cheryl Pelow's vivid paintings on the walls. Cheryl did the pictures for my chapbook, *The Moon Card*, in 2001, and I have brought well-wrapped copies to complement her show.

Dawna, the proprietor, greets me from behind the counter and gives me tea. A couple of guitarists are riffing quietly; a few other people are sitting over warm drinks and late lunches.

"I've got artists, I've got musicians," Dawna says as she tells me her dreams for the café. "All I need are poets."

"I know poets," I offer. "I could arrange a reading or two."

Walking home in the snow, night already and not yet five o'clock, I realize I know quite a lot of poets. The list starts to sprawl. I choose more experienced, often better-known writers to anchor each reading and ask them who they'd like to read with. I try to arrange the readings in clusters, by friendship, association, mentoring relationship. After a short time, I've arranged seven readings (an eighth emerges later), beginning in February with some of Kingston's best, Joanne Page and Helen Humphreys, and ending in May with three of Kingston's best – Mary Cameron, Jason Heroux and Steven Heighton. I know I haven't asked every existing Kingston poet – this is a reading series after all, not a poetic licence – but I've asked writers whose work I find interesting and alive or writers other writers in the series find interesting. The list ranges from former students in their 20s to poets in their 70s and early 80s, all from the Kingston area.

The first reading is Friday, February 11. The café is packed. Sandra Davies, who is giving her first reading, has brought her writing group. Joanne Page has put the notice out to Georgette Fry's choir. People have come to hear Helen Humphreys; others have come to hear Paul Kelley, little known in Kingston. Dawna's assistants keep bringing more chairs; there is a long lineup for coffee and tea; some people are sitting on the floor and standing. Edna Alford has said that the Kingston literary community is the envy of everyone in Canada – this expectant crowd, including writers, readers, friends, and relatives, seems proof of it.

Margaret Little begins to play the piano; Joanne reads water and ice poems to Margaret's lyric, fluid accompaniment. We all hush with being inside the moment.

Sandra reads her poems about her mother's last illness. Paul reads his elegant, polished poems. Helen gives her own black comedy version of the northern sea voyage that inspired Joanne's work and reads a wonderful piece about the library of the Franklin Expedition, about books, the imagination, knowing writers through books. As the reading ends, we're all filled with words, images, ideas, music, renewed energy.

Not all the readings are so jammed to the rafters, but they all have that buzz of discovery, hearing new work, or previously unknown work, in the poet's own voice.

No book can recreate a series of readings, especially the readings that included music, but included in these pages are almost all the poets who read. These are the writers we share the streets with, meet at the Market, or at the Sleepless Goat. With minor variations, I have tried to reflect the arrangement of the series and the "clusters" of the readings in the order of the book.

Both the reading series and the book have been truly collective enterprises, drawing their beings from the generosity of the poets' community. My deepest thanks to the poets for contributing their time, energy and wonderful words to bring both to life. Special thanks to Laurie Lewis, who envisioned this book and gave it shape.

Kingston Poets' Gallery does not attempt to be exhaustive. There are many other poets in Kingston, both published and unpublished. But this book does include our poets of national and international reputation as well as many emerging writers worth watching. This is a generous sample of the poetry being written in our community. Ezra Pound said "I have gathered from the air a live tradition." This is our live tradition, varied and vibrant.

Good writing gives us back our world with vision cleared, and I hope many of these poems do that for you, the readers.

Elizabeth Greene
Kingston, February 2006

AN APPRECIATION

This book is the result of Elizabeth Greene's generosity and arises, in part, from the breadth of her life in Kingston. An accomplished writer and editor, Elizabeth drew upon her fellow poets in the community for the reading series she organized and hosted at the Gallery Café in the winter and spring of 2005. With the addition of emerging poets she discovered in her literature classes and those she found further afield, the Friday afternoon readings were fresh, unpredictable and often drew standing-room-only crowds. In all, twenty-eight poets took part in the series. Most appear in the pages that follow. It is entirely in keeping with Elizabeth's enthusiasm and reach that she would not only conceive an ambitious series but would ensure its permanence by shepherding the words into print. Poetry could not have a better friend.

HELEN HUMPHREYS AND JOANNE PAGE

Kingston Poets' Gallery

JOANNE PAGE

Disco Bay, Greenland

Pitch and yaw in open water, ice forest in sight against a
    parchment sky,
dominions of winter calve off the ice field at Ilulissat in August.
We hurry to the deck in sea jackets and winter gear, flock of eager
    puffins,
our ship a company of pairs: Jesuits, cardiologists, Sicilian twins,
Manhattan shrinks, hand-writing analysts, a couple of farmers
    from Komoka,
as if Noah had put the passenger list together with a view to
    preserving
the less common specimens of the species by freezing.

Now we are eggs in a carton, a dozen at a time push off in
    motorized rafts,
tiny scarlet spots among the continents of ice, damp exhalations of
    frigid air rise from
each like prehistoric breathing. The boatman stills the engine. We
    drift.
He tells of penguins lined up at the edge of the ice in Antarctica
(where the rest of the freshwater is stored) all shuffling sideways
    nudging
one off to feed the waiting leopard seal so the rest may dive. We
    lock eyes
in our opposing rows, here at the beginning of the world or the
    end.

Toward Baffin

Pocked and rippled the great bergs sail north
on their bands of neon melt. They are rose

blue, green, even peach, a Fifth Avenue
in ice loosed in the Gulf Stream, in and out

of the fog they come and go, antique dreams
like the practice of high courtesy we now name love.

Overhead the dovkies, pint-sized beer cans with wings
in millions on their summer flight to Lancaster Sound.

Is this a lesson of emptiness or optics, the law of averages
or motion? We are dots on the deck of our shabby ship

in our so-called expedition gear, the boat a speck in a sea
of floating behemoths that can sink us by merely overturning

in a moment too small in time for history.
The only insanity is not to be afraid.

Beside me you want your car to appear on the next floe,
voyage of doom, you hiss, keys in your hand,

undone by magnitude of scale. *Voyage of light,*
I think, a way to make life and death weightless.

Davis Strait

Here we go to up the coast in company with floating archipelagos
borealis azure, parliaments of ice boating north and west to Canada,
lordly tourists, motherlands with hitchhikers, gulls, seals,
the occasional white bear, the world in a guise I had imagined
but did not know to be a question: If this is not your Eden
what is?

I would require seasons, five or six, and a book of words to use
with one set of meanings, I would need pure colour
in great sweeps as well as inside and underneath where
you don't expect it. Belief would take the form of tolerant irony,
say lapsed Quaker, lack temple priests and rules but one:
love when you can.

My Eden would run on marsh gas, on wind, be governed by those
who mean to save the world with zeal except for Texans or,
come to think of it, feminist collectives, its civic spaces
made of dance and song and public art of the impermanent kind
that announces itself by departing. My Eden would have some hot
dark nights,

insects, frogs, roosting orange birds, ripe fruit, free lunch,
stable money and hauls of harvest, fair play, invention,
clean wells, children in bed linen by open windows and snow,
yes, now and then on the domed roofs of the capital, at the edge
of the sea where the white bear swims on his back through the bright
night of his hunt.

Desperation Lake, NWT
or Unrequited Love

When there's no facing it down or fencing it in,
when you can't be cured, when you discover yourself
among small rodents haring down a worn path
repeatedly signed *this way to the cliff*, when
you are the overheated one in a temperate zone
or fail to notice the boom of your voice too loud
and off-key when the piece is over.

If after a lifelong comfort in reckless declaration
you fall into cramped speech, if a regular vow
to contain the huge and apparently raucous burden
of your emotional carnival vies with a pledge to tear aside
the veil behind which you deliberately hide, if baggage-
talk does not mean tryst or even a two-day jaunt
and you dare not go alone for fear the tide might turn,

oh dear, the last place you need is a quiet pond, all that reflection
and night echo, or a river's promise of arrival. Grab field
glasses for the long view, a level for balance. Imagine yourself
small in a big landscape, say the tundra, with its hundred
thousand lakes and inch-high flowers in unheard of variety.
Consider being stuck with one. Now study the rock. Faced with
      stone
not even the moon's might can bring to ebb what never flowed.

SANDRA DAVIES

Poems for my lost mother
prologue

Regrets
December 25, 2003

There is no way to fix this.

My mother is ninety-six
and lives in a facility,
genteel, Catholic,
caregivers who often
really care.

I put her there some
months ago when
she blindly fell
and smashed
her little hip.

She's killed me off,
thinks I'm dead,
weeps for me
from time to time,
but mostly lashes out.

Or sits silent. Lost
in her wheelchair
she doesn't even know
that it's Christmas.
Or that I miss her.

#10, March 30, 2005

My birthday, sixty-five, a big one. People say
it's just a number, but it isn't.
It scares me, this descent to senior status.
They'll give me money just because I'm old.
Am I useless now, needing handouts,
 powers dwindling? Will my health fail soon, my mind?

I take a chance, go to see my mother.
She sits in her wheelchair, feet propped up as usual,
skeletal and absent, her mouth working constantly.
No sound. Sometimes she does this. She mouths to me
that she is tired – I've learned to read her lips.
The nurses tell me she is quiet, good, complacent.

She won't open her eyes. I'm proud, and I tell her
that her grandson, my youngest, is teaching in Toronto.
She speaks! "That lazy bum – he always liked to sit
down on his ass! Teachers don't do anything! Zero!"
Even in dementia, she knows how to strike.
Defeated, I can't tell her it's my birthday.

Better just to leave it all alone.
I lose the battle with my reddening eyes, weep
in utter silence, long to rest my head
down on her shoulder,
feel her cool soft fingers on my cheek.
Tell her that I'm old. Have her fix it.

#11, April 25, 2005

Sweet kisses today, and gentle patting all over my face,
the way a baby does when its mother comes into view.
She's happy to see whoever she thinks I am. I wait.
Did you know my mother, Lillie-Anne? she asks.
There's a hyphen. She smiles, delighted with herself.
Then corrects. No hyphen. Lilianne. She was your
favorite grandma. So she knows me. Don't blow it.

I tell her that I do remember well, and I wonder if
a story will emerge. But she pauses for a breath, then
asks about the weather, and my oldest son, and something
new, a mystery man, a black man, with whom she thinks I
share my home. It used to be her greatest fear, that I would
run away with someone on my *list of ethnic boyfriends*. I
don't argue now. Tell her he's fine, that everything's OK.

She's off again, smiling. A happy little story for her daughter.
Tells me that her father was transported down the other day.
Taken from his heavenly home on high by an angel, white
and tall, who pushed him in a wheelchair. He came to see her
acting in a play, with nothing for a script, so she had to make
it up. "An 'ad lib' play," she marvels. Holds my hand in hers.
Tells me that he loved her in it. "Clapped and clapped!" she says.

I don't know where her brain goes any more,
but today there is a lightness. She needs to
see her daddy, and she simply serves him up. She needs to
love her daughter, and she smiles and pats my face.
She wants to bless us all, and she does.
I hope she dies like this.

I see her now, kneeling in the earth.
She's peering over her glasses
at three tiny crocus cups.

She turns to me, beaming.
Just look at these little miracles,
she says.

For My Friend Berta After Her Departure

You told me fervently that you had a good life,
"Just not enough of it," you said, and we both cried.
I held your hands and we sat together in the quiet,
in some corner of the peace that
we thought you would never find.

Later, all skin and bones, you could hardly sit,
and I placed your arms around my neck –
lifted you, at your insistence, to the commode.
Barely able to speak, you grinned at me.
"I'm peeing," you said. "Not dead yet."

Later still, when I held you, your chest shuddering with
the effort of breath, you asked straight out if you were dying.
"Pretty soon, my love," I said, and asked if you were scared.
I pressed my ear to hear your whisper. "Not of dying…"
"Then what?" I asked, desperate to have you go without fear.

"Of pain, that awful goddam pain. Like my mother. At the end."
I found your ear with my mouth. "Oh honey, oh my sweetheart,
oh Berta," I said your name. We have the morphine here. There
won't be any pain." A breathy laugh from you. "Well, if you're
right," you said, I'll fly straight over your house. Let you know."

Two o'clock in the morning, I'm suddenly awake.
Sit up in bed. Feel you speeding by.
Know you've gone now.
No pain for you.
Not for you.

HELEN HUMPHREYS

Hurricane

We waited all evening for it,
with candles and beer, in the unfinished
part of the house. All around us the slow
progress of your new life – everything still exposed,
the stiff uprights that would support the walls,
the nests of wire.

We gave up, went to bed, and then I heard you scream
when the tree fell behind the house, missing it
by inches. When we opened the back door, a mesh
of leaves covered our faces. We went out then,
unwisely, into the swirling wind and the bright
green sky, the pop of transformers blowing, and

the entrails of wires dripping from the trees.
The wind was wild above us and we walked
below in a canopy of stillness. You are lucky,
although you would never say that about yourself,
but the night had spared your house, your car,
your boyfriend's truck, the plans you have together.

The streets smelled of wet, green wood. Huge
trees had fallen in an instant, each still shod
in a giant, earthen slipper, leaning wearily
into each other or resting on a sagging net of wires.
How hard it is to know what is the new life
and what is the world ending.

Foxes

I'm reading poems by a woman who wrote about
her death before she knew she was dying. Poetry
rises as memory, comes down as prophesy.

What I wanted was to tell the story of the foxes.
The drive up, before dawn, to see the sun rise
behind the lighthouse. How the two foxes circled us

in the parking lot, one jumping onto the car and peeing,
staring at us through the windshield, defiant and sure,
red fur lit with wind. How afterwards everyone

said this shouldn't have happened, this behaviour, these
foxes at the lighthouse. But I don't know where
to end this story, and what I'm really doing is

reading, not writing. Better to be in the dead poet's
poems about haystacks and pears, than to be here,
in the mountains, or to be here, in the poem.

In the mountains early snow has blanched the summer
grass and the woods at night blaze like an x-ray.
In the poem there are black rocks by the road

As we drive up to the lighthouse. Blossoms of fog
bloom once, lush and flawless against the glass.
There we tried to read the foamy alphabet

of the sea, the cold, salt air tasting of secrets.
We wanted the right word for everything. Here,
the dead poet talks about the woods, but they're not

these woods. Reading her puts me where I am and
takes me from there too. The pull of it
like wanting. (Ten years ago I would have said

desire, but that's not it.) Wanting is a word that fills
and empties, a word that, like the sea, remembers
itself each time differently.

At first we were certain the foxes were a warning.
Then we thought that somehow they were us. The
menace was ourselves, each other. Now I think

it's all true. There was a sluice of light
behind them on the hills as they ran through the dry
grass, away from us. And you have gone now,

just as swiftly. Well, goodbye. I want to say
that what we did, trying to name the fog on the hills,
was like writing, but not as lonely. It was like

reading, not lonely at all. And the foxes.
What they've become now are words – these ones, the ones
of the dead poet. They circled us and left us.

Grief and consolation. Mercy, mercy, like a rope of stars.
This is the space between fire and sea, between
what I know and what I can say.

And I have always told myself that I live
for this – what comes for me
and is not mine.

Appetite

That was the name of those stones on the table,
capsules of blue so small that at first
I thought they were berries. This was after dinner.
I pulled the dish over and rattled their hard shine.

This was after I'd played a game of horseshoes
with my host and accidentally thrown a red horseshoe
into the lake. The next day my best friend said
it was lucky to have done this, and this is how

I knew she loved me. We couldn't find it with the rake.
The lake was too weedy. And supper was spaghetti,
which looked like more weeds on my plate.
The light came on. The light went off. The lake

was still, a dark blue, the colour of appetite.
On the way home I sobbed in the car, fearing
you'd leave me, not knowing what to believe – the time
you said, "Have faith in me," or the time you said, "Fuck love."

If appetite were that easy, that manageable. If I could
split a geode when I needed to be hungry. If it was
something that happened outside my body, something I could
pick up and put down whenever I wanted,
something still and stone and cold.

P A U L   K E L L E Y

Four poems from "Aweathered"

i

Cloud-shelled
whispers of our wandering,
our irregular music
the autumn mists enfold,
half-light, much,
roomed in the stone.

And half-hopes, many,
for our murmurings,
our fallen prayers,
the darkness absorbs.
The weight of the flowers
press us into ourselves.

Earth-worn,
dumbed by praising mouths:
the light of a name
buried back to its source.
Memory's ends ignite there
the convulsive birth of this start.

For Ines and Marlene
1-2 November, 2003
All Saints' Day / All Souls' Day
Vienna

ii

Perched on the tip of the thorn,
come cradled in moonlight,
in sheets of tide and stone: silence
binds each clod to the spark of a star,

bares this moment as the ever when
histories begin their motions
                and their rests:

one pulse worth all the pain
of having been born.

For Karen Dubinsky
31 January, 2004
Havana

iii
Two inseparable aspects of present space

The bay of remembrance
we crossed at full dark,
guided by the loosed light finding us
in the there, in the vast between;
liquid our element will be,
and by its laws we will swear,
with the shudderings under
of oceans and engines,

within each of us a cargo of self
where we arrive,
at pasts ago and pasts afore,
where we arrive –
at the swell and the drop of uncertain delivery

*

To behold the glimmer of the isle,
clotted with clouds and the cold kiss of them,
wakens once a host of happy chances –
of hills and rock, of their histories
of the hands of the eyes of the backs – theirs,
not ours – bending and lifting and placing,
to together their days.

And a small sun atop the high ladder
– yesterday, was it –
its rungs numberless as the waves
scaling from this end the deeps of the sky.

For Susan Belyea

iv
On Inis Mór

Think of the storm that rages in the glass,
the knot in the air at your throat.

In your pocket, a splinter of a past not your own
rolled smooth in pools of the sea,
saved, not lost, at this edge for your plucking:

call it porcelain,
call it China,
call it a gift.

A surface, without substance or shape,
for a thoughtful hand to hold to.

Once it was:
call it time.

For Helen
18 December 2003
Dundalk, County Louth

Eric Folsom

Northeast

If you picked any story but this,
I wouldn't know where to begin.

The grey November sky predicting early snow,
The ground already resisting footprints.

A young doe in my garden looks up;
How the mind seeing, loses sight.

Inside where I stand, one cobweb on the ceiling
Delicately twists when the furnace comes to life.

What if I turned my face away
And when I looked back you were gone?

The freezing mud in the driveway
Seizes the tires in their ruts overnight.

I wish for multiple eyes like a spider,
My forehead of shining cobblestones.

The Gore

Clay mud whitens as it dries on the tires,
Patterned grooves left in the driveway.

Beyond the last field, a dense swamp under starlight;
He calls them coyotes, wild dogs his own answers.

Strength enough left to shore up the old house,
He knows that old barns fall down mainly at night.

Next farm west, facing the highway,
The big sign announces a planned community.

No fish could live in a stream this small,
Though salmon were once plentiful in the harbour.

If he looks sharp, he sees a fox
Cutting through his orchard in the morning.

This cup is full, so easy to spill;
No love without wanting, no power without control.

Slipping Away

Whatever lies frozen in the ice, a mitten or a Buick,
Suspended as though floating upside down in the sky.

The fiddle music over, so the priest went home
And saw the ghost of his father sitting on the bed.

Late in the season when the ice gets soft,
Some drunk tries to cross at night and disappears.

Most people worry about saying the wrong thing,
Think too long about the darkness beneath their feet.

Wheels lock automatically
When passenger doors are open.

She gave her daughter the red sweater and a key
To the safety deposit box down at the bank.

Something that shouldn't have been there,
A car in the same spot for days, gathering tickets.

Natural History

"Create with form, not line," said the art teacher,
"build with masses of light and dark."

Gradually plants evolved from gymnosperm to seed
And the Age of Flowers dawned on the Earth.

I forget the dead sometimes, leave them out of poems,
And they come back in dreams to remind me.

My grandmother spoke to me when I was nine,
"You won't forget your mother will you?"

The seeds of the new plants made concentrated food,
Allowing birds and mammals to evolve and flourish.

I'm running out of energy, lesson plan falling apart;
"What do we mean," I say twice, "by economy?"

Any world is dangerous and filled with metaphor:
The burning lasers of our eyes, fatal wounds of birth.

ERIN FOLEY

The Thing That Endures
For Virginia Woolf

You appeared to me once
in a dream
offering a bouquet of roses.
Your lips parted to speak
my enthusiasm cut you off.
You smiled and turned away.
I watched your shape float from me
imagining the taste of your mind,
I wanted to touch your ink stained fingers

but this moment is all.

What is it you wanted to say
before my passion cut you short?
What is it you could not say
except through the weight of stones,
the press of water?
Drowned by vision – falling deeper still
you triumph
you had not said it: yet I knew.

Call Me Crazy

"I'm in love with myself," you say,
laugh and then call me crazy.
I smile
an attempt to hide
chipped nail polish and sucked in gut.
Your unapologetic poetry makes me feel
not good enough.

I saw myself in the window
while we spoke.
Your sharp flow of words
absurd against the roundness of my mind.
I tried to outshine you
with grandiose gestures and purple hair
was left sinking –
the weight of ridiculous.

A victim of catch and release logic
dividing against myself
because of your short skirts
and polished Doc Martens.
Studying the words
you try to describe the way
black strokes on a white page
can change your life.

But is it worth it?

A greater change possible
with my breath upon your ear
lips devouring the language of rising breast,
tongue on collar bone,
the dialects of crumpled sheets.

I watch you float in your body
a comfort I will never know.
You explain,
"everyone should be in love
with me."
I smile again and look away,

I like it when you call me crazy.

Fuck the Secretary of Defense

Turned on CNN
hoping to catch a glimpse.
There's something sexy about the way
you can answer a question
by not answering the question.
The circular logic of "us" and "them"
spun around the axis of evil.
I'm convinced Republicans have better sex
and I'm dying for you to show me.
I unbutton my pants and spread my legs,
I can't help myself
curious about what's hidden behind the podium.
I imagine you taking me in each wing of the Pentagon.
That's right, all five.
Something charmingly smug about you
can't put my finger on it…
I bite my lip and listen to you talking dirty
freedom and war on terror and weapons of mass destruction
stars and stripes and red and white oh you'll need that little blue
   pill.
We'll make Clinton look like a choir boy.
I want you out of office and into my bed.
Politics don't matter when you're naked.
Those lying lips make me hot
and I want them all over my body.
It doesn't matter that you're responsible for Aspartame
or that your hair has been the same for thirty years.
I watch your big, strong hands and slow my rhythm
imagine their expertise
bound to have learned some moves in seventy-two years.
I only hope it's a slow news day
and we can meet again on NewsNight with Aaron Brown.

M. E. CSAMER

Dying looked at me today

out of the eyes of a dead squirrel
said   *I'm coming, wait for me.*
I realized I had been
and stopped.

Since her dying
my mother has moved in with me.
I carry her, pick-a-back into the future,
what was rich and needful in her life
now mine.

The weapons we have against dying
are carried in the flesh: weapons
of bone, the heart, a bowl
full of memory and bones, the hands
growing the shape of their ancestors', slight
arthritic ache begins to turn
the fingers in: beggars' hands
their
permanent wanting.

Electric
live wire squirrels in the park,
acrobatic
tree hoppers, nut casers
but not hard
nuts to crack:

dying got one of you today.

I would have said death
but it's not the same, is it?

My mother has been dead two years:
a history,
a dwelling,   a marker, a memory,

but her dying, oh,
that was an event.

Pierre

I found a maple leaf on the sidewalk this morning:
solitary
ironic three points turned east,
colour vivid but aging. Frost
had already begun the black band around the edges.

It wanted a river
somewhere to flow effortlessly
into turbulence, match
strength for strength
in honest, if artful, battle.

But there was only that grey cement
hard, mathematically measured into precise
squares: a logical route to the next place.

So I stepped into the street
where maple keys in the gutter
spoke to the mess of Fall,
that passionate letting go.

Maureen

In the old coffee shop
of the psychiatric hospital
sound leaks through the walls
from the new cafeteria;
this room, like me, redundant now
the ex-patient sipping tea,
watching the sold out lights
on the coin machine blinking.

Two interns by the microwave
await their warming lunches
talking future plans, a jogging date.
Smugness starched into their coats,
the white of arrival.

One rests his hand on the table
where you sat that night
between your parents, their grave faces
an odd frame to your laughter.

I see you still, Maureen,
inhaler in hand, that peculiar teddy bear.
Hooked on the feel of it, you said
magic air for wheezing lungs
you thought had outgrown the need.

Did I speak your name out loud?
The interns stiffen, look around.
Is it ghosts they fear?

But there's no haunting here.
Your death lies quietly,
a book in my hand
turned to the last page

its mystery unsolved:
asthma or suicide?

I'll never know.
This book is no whodunit.
This book's a life,
eighteen little pages
wild with wanting

soft laughter spilling back.

TARA KAINER

Late Bloomer

You took all summer.

Potted flowers I bought
in the spring sat
dormant on the fire escape
through gentle rains
and hot, hazy days
while all around
trees burst
into leaf, and
below,
in the garden,
tulips and daffodils,
peonies and cosmos,
rushed headlong
to glory.

You sat still
unperturbed
your ragged
foliage upturned
and smiling
while fruits withered
on the vine, leaves
browned and curled,
you emerged, round
tight buds at first,
then a steady
unfolding: tiny
white petals,
luminous

centers,
a plethora
of suns fringed
by a blazing corona.

Now grey day crowds
in around you, the
punishing wind rises:
you hold on. Wintry
nights press close,
time is short, but oh!
so precious
you
white queen
of the moonlight
bearing your
white
chrysanthemum
truth
ancient as Confucious
ubiquitous as the wind
are rooted to your place
high above
the garden
of those
blackened,
impassioned
flowers.

It's the laughter

It's the laughter
in the evening –
Dolores & June
sprawled in their
lawn chairs across
the street, taking
a well-deserved
rest after 60-odd
years of feminine
struggle, calling
Howdy stranger! as
I step out the door
into the lengthening
shadows of the deepening
day: it's the murmur
of their voices as I
pick tomatoes hanging
like moons; it's the
moon, high & full
racing past clouds
the colour of dust
& ripe blueberries,
the call of the geese
in V-formation, my
cats in the garden
crouched low, stalking
their neighbours; it's
the wind, the cool
lake breeze sweeping
across the land
to my yard, lifting
my clothes & my hair
with its soft, gentle
fingers, balm to
the pressing white
heat of the day: it's

gathering ripe tomatoes
like jewels in my arms,
offering the treasures
to June & Delores who
give me recipes & praise
in exchange;

it's their
asking, Do you know
what marijuana looks
like? Then leading
me to the edge
of the street to
point at a plant, a
leprechaun green,
frayed-edged, three-
leafed gem springing
up from the pavement, &
me saying, It sure
looks like marijuana;
their hoots of laughter,
confessing they hadn't
believed Jason but
they do me, yet how could
it be, where did it
come from, who could
have planted the seed?
it's their warning me
in conspiratorial giggles
I might see them stumbling
& acting queer; it's
hearing their voices
fade away in the
dusk as I ascend
my apartment stairs,
tomato-laden & light-
hearted; oh, yes, it's
the laughter
in the evening.

HOLLAY GHADERY

Tongue Rising
(coup against the cardiac)

He tells me that I have three types of muscle and Cardiac, my
    heart, is a special one. I
can't help but feel that my heart gets too much attention. Has been
    – is – revered enough.
Enough.
Yes, enough already. Just stop.

No,
not my heart, but the fixation with that plump, impassioned
    pound of flesh. What about
my tongue?
Strongest muscle in my body. Can clear-cut rainforests of rhetoric
    like a child cuts right
to the point and leaves you
blushing – scurrying under skirts of *ums* and *ohs*. Avoiding
    questions. No,
answers. Awkward moments that put you face to tongue with
    something unpleasant and yes,
vaguely familiar – Bittersweet

is licking the sweat off his stomach. I have the tongue but not the
    heart to tell him I've never come
to the same conclusions.
Tongues do all the work and hearts fall silent.

Tongue,
Pumping proverbial iron. Oooooh, that primordial power. That
riveting, rippling flex.
Dream waking, love making muscle. Yes –

a slip of the tongue can break any heart.

Quine Does Couples Therapy

Persistent and stubborn, Quine has kept me up all night,
lecturing me on love and pointing a steady finger at the source
of our weakness. Hand on my heart, he says
this is why you are destined to fail
raps on my head and tells me
this isn't just for show, you know

He has cringed at every proclamation, pronounced us *fools!*
what do you know of truth? what
do you love more than yourself?
Slammed his fist on the desk and declared *you make love*
to a word and
expect it to fight the world out of your bedroom

Come morning, I'm
red eyed,
sleep-deprived,
tongue lashed
into proverbial love with another man

I'm behind his desk,
on his lap,
lips against his ear
telling him
this isn't just for show,
you know.

counting in Alberta

I'm this

a girl listening to Alberta, circling the sky

running the coulees with arms holding
one hundred hours

at twenty-four, I've expected nothing, but I'm
more now, in the free air and cow shit,
with the highway unfolding below and tasting
one hundred ends, traveling at
different speeds

I've been this girl one hundred times
before

running
the coulees in Alberta

I'm this

at twenty-four, ten sheets to the wind,
winding one hundred hours round the coulees,
into this: one.

Christmas Lights in October
(a temporal study)

They ripped that dress he loved so much, the one
with slits up to her hips, neckline down
to her navel. The one she wore that night with
the *fuck me* shoes in the middle of October; before
the first snowfall and during the last downpour.
The one she wore that night he drove six hours
in the rain, just to fall at her feet, naked
while she did the dishes in a haze of Christmas lights
in October. He promised her then –
tucking her hair behind her ear then fucking her
when she knelt down to kiss him –
He promised her then that three years later
she'd never be now. She remembers how
he promised her then, forever when
she was elbow deep in dishes and dreaming
of a better life – drowning in October.

It isn't until she sticks that picture on her mirror –
(that one they took that night she wore that dress
he loved so much) –
that she sees then facing her
now and remembers when
she stopped feeling December the same way.

LOUISE O'DONNELL

Nostalgia

Sometimes nostalgia hits
like a fist in the throat.

How can it be that three tumbling decades
have passed since you split open the
I'm fine, thank you very much, lie of my life.

The new grade five teacher
practicing his guitar in a corner of my office.
Gentle chords to smooth the chaos
at the end of day after hectic day.
When did I comprehend that I was being serenaded?
How long could I deny the time spent analyzing
Marx's Theory of Surplus Value
long after the school emptied, was more than
help with my evening courses.

Certainly not after that student arrived at my door,
presented a stapled sheet of newsprint
bearing the title *Ode on a Grecian Urn,*
its contents having nothing whatever
to do with a Grecian Urn.

What a parade of faces appear in nostalgia's eye
as you settle into a chair, and with your new guitar,
fill our kitchen with soft chords.

Excursions

Outside my window the lake
is hurling ice rocks against the shore
then greedily retrieving shards
as ammunition for its next assault.
Inside my fire burns low.
As I contemplate a trip to the woodpile
my eyes scan the room, drink in
souvenirs from days spent far from winter.
They come to rest on a tall blue vase
over painted with gold filigree and delicate petals.
The lake's roar recedes.

I am in a closet sized room in Jiangmen City,
The People's Republic of China.
It is evening. Through the single window
come mosquitoes to nosedive our ears
and moths to create lazy circles we, distracted,
will brush away with waving arms.
Four young women and one
equally young man have come
to honour me with the gift of their words.
Together we fashion magical places,
create other selves more wise and
more daring than we,
make friends with the moon
who was lonely in her starless sky.
And through our laughter we make a compact.

At least once each year we will soar
to the other side of reality
meet in places reachable only by following
the map etched in our collective dreams.

I take down their parting gift,
let my fingers trace its shape,
begin a journey to a place where
only the initiated can interpret the landscape.

Decide against a trip to the woodpile,
there is warmth enough in this room.

Titania's Jewelry

Walk softly now,
create no stir.
Quickly mind,
before the sun lights all her candles.

Night's artistry is on display.
Spread between a sapling's fragile tips,
dewdrops strung on spider silk:
fine jewelry fit to grace the neck
of proud Titania.

Poem for Alli

Azure sky shot through
with salmon coloured cloud,
lighthouse on the point
blinking its welcome/warning.
Lake Ontario
whispering to shoreside rocks,

and a single green canoe
bearing an orange life jacket,
lilliputian size, and
a daddy, patient beyond belief
introducing his dark haired beauty
to the quiet game of tease and pull
played with the lake's inhabitants.

Tomorrow you will fly
home to far Japan. Twelve more
months before you will again
grace us with your tiny exuberance.
Someday in the distant future
there might be portraits:
you in a long white veil,
a loving gaze exchanged.
A new generation on its way,

but me, I'll see
a green canoe, an orange jacket,
and Lake Ontario, gentle as you go.

MARIE LLOYD

The Dead are Never Greedy

The dead are never greedy –
clouds will do for angels, or
these seagulls,
and a single full moon's
infinite enough.
        No ballast anymore,
no hunger. Heaven's
anyplace, even at your
side as you down cereal
or as you wash the deck
or drop a softball.
        They're too generous,
too free of matter to
remember,
so their love for us
is perfect and elastic.
For example
in these breathy winds
among the cedars
Claire is holding Sancho, but
we are always eating
losing something
moving elsewhere and
forgetting to look down
to look more closely –

Forest Story

In the glade, her glass
coffin rests against an oak.
Today it is attended by a fly
rubbing its prickled hands in
unwilled prayer.

　No one comes anymore –
the dwarves, faithful for a time
at last have tired of the misted
glass, the glints of sunlight
off that box that
burnt the eyes and left only
the rare too-bright glance of red
samite, the mirage of raven hair
seeming on fire –

　tricks of moonlight, too,
levelling the thing inside and
what was out, the lambent
mushrooms just as pale
and yielding as her open mouth,
then the duplicitous mouth itself
a smear of lichen dark on rounded rock.

　The Prince we think
was seized by fairies, or has
unwisely eaten elvish bread –
if released, he is too late:
aging and blinded, fine cloak rent,
even now, even as we speak
his hands are withering
his fingers reach like whispers
in among these shifting trees.

Fire Keeps Going

One sidelong look –
a soft blur of burning orchard, then
the hard glance of fire on iron.

Eve sees
something like a fawn ignite,
its thin churning legs glow
like spokes on a Catherine wheel.

Now against her shoulder,
the touch of charred wing, dark
and falling. Now she feels it –
rapture – for the first time. And
this terror's thin vibrato, as
when at dusk a nestling
calls to the long snake face.

Eve remembers,
pulls at her incandescent hair – embers,
embers. She's invented all this,
and that sound –
the clangor of a final
dark portcullis
as the sun falls.

She's brought night, too,
from her shut lids and the
insides of her body.

Now Eve looks back,
watches the first of the ones
who've left and followed,
they, too, loose and burnt and dazzled,
moving in the rudiments of line.

GABRIELLE MCINTIRE

Summer Surprised Us

I have come this way
To the whispery waxy island entreaties
Of late-summer cricket songs and blackbirds' play
Where golden-brown sun-warmed beauty
Today rests, watchful but reposing,
Mellow, under the last true blue sky
Of the season's late closing,
Haven for one light, shimmer, ripple-drawn dragonfly.

I have seen a counterpointed
Complimentary purple-ringing flower
Set beneath a yellow leaf, annointed
With the too-late summer's fading power
Its conjoinery, its October
Bridging the end point of heat and light
With the start of Autumn's might,
The opening of yellow, the glowing over.

I have seen cormorants with their black bills
Pointed to the heavens, arrows of desire,
A mimicry of this morning's one hundred geese in skilled
Formation, honking, plucking on the lyre
Of this heart's too-taught strings
Asking for an undoing, an unlearning, a tuning
To the never-wearied press for sun and moon
And all things beating out the span of life on wings.

Shivering Ash on the Edge of Ramsden Park

Pale green silver shimmering underside
Of those leaves bending in the wind
Like a high and fine billowing blaze,
Kindled in an instant at an astonishing height –
The face of things to come.
Shuddering, dancing, waving its braided body,
The tree's loosened tresses,
Its gentleness reborn
With the breath of midsummer's being,
Sounding terribly far and
Terribly near to this heart's
Vermilion-gushing trembling care.

My eye catches such a dance
From below just when all dancing
Seems through, and breathing
A labour simply of staying –
Of not letting the washed-out wastes of time
Be finished with me yet.

And then the sudden joy-flash
That overcomes even the darkest coursing
Thoughts, the saddest inner moiled tunes,
And floods my senses with a momentary rapture
At this infinitesimally small portion, tide-moment,
Of the heaving and rolling perennial loveliness
Of the spirit-as-world.
The sky meeting earth
Through the outstretched arms
Of green.

Break Through

The ice broke today
At 11:53 a.m., Eastern Standard Time –
Suddenly a runnel-rivulet of blue
Opened up between the white thighs
Of ice.
We had walked on water
Just days ago,
Confident of the solid support
Of "eight inches thick,"
Sealed and unemotional,
A bridge between the mainland and the islands.

I've been waiting, watching,
Wondering when the water's inner
Boil would need to break free –
And then it was just so suddenly there,
This morning – a blue flat field
Of spring calm, winter-framed:
Blue on white,
Deep blue, perfect white.

And then the field burst a trickle
And a river started to creep
Toward the shore, meandering,
The sun finally having gotten through.

I missed it, the happening,
I didn't see the instant of the crack.
Only the darkish shadows under a thinning surface
Hinted to me this morning
That the breaking point had come.

It's been nine weeks since I saw you,
Oh waters of blue.
I've missed you, I've anticipated a dream,
I've waited for your movement,
Opus 34,
Stagione primavera –
In 4/4 time,
Allegro, molto.

ELIZABETH GREENE

Five a.m on Gore Street, August 2004

Five a.m – there's a great yellow dinosaur
Outside my window, lurid in street light.
It's digging up the past: rust-encrusted pipes,
Old dirt, old stone – and putting down the future.
Enormous hand attached to squat yellow body,
treads for feet, scoops up cement and rubble.

By seven all these huge machines will start
Rolling back and forth, ungainly barnyard chicks
Beeping and squeaking as if they're speaking
Martian. Jackhammers drilling down through
Iron-tinted dirt, through limestone shelves
To pipes that allow our lives to flow
Water in, sewer out.

But at 5 a.m. they're tame, these yellow giants
So misnamed cats – no fur, no purr, all work, no play –
My cats walk between their giant treads
Before the whole day is smashed with noise.

Through the rubble, along the chasms of the torn-up street
A broad-beamed skunk, huge white stripe
Down his back, plumy tail, waving like a false truce,
Scuttles forward, short-legged, undaunted, tough.
"I was here before this fuss began. I'll be here when it's done."

The Haunted Walk

Suddenly we're kids again
Scurrying, leaf-scuffing, through the velvet night
Under the slanting silver of the October moon.

Like Halloween, but here the treat's
All tricks. Our black-cloaked guide
Lifts her small lantern, holds us in a group

And as she talks, our daily rounds are changed.
We're in a timeless space, the world of story,
The world of restless ghosts who hold

Some of these stone houses still.
At night they hover above these angled streets
Unquiet spirits who never did resolve

Black angers, grasping hates, unfinished lives.
They move in winter cold no fire can warm
Rattle plates and windows, knock on walls

Asking us to bring them to the light
The only way they know. They live with knives,
Some cutting throats; some touch our shoulders

Begging the kindness that their deaths denied.
Our spines chill. How easy it would be
To stumble into some ghost's house or story.

What would you do? Try to sleep with rattling
saying, "Wake!" Call an exorcist or simply flee?
Or put out milk, or wine, to make your peace?

Suddenly we're back where we began
Emerge from past to present, from bones
and spirit to breath and blood.

We walk home singly
Under the risen moon and
Vow to light a candle for the dead.

Bronwen's Lemon Balm

Fourteen years later
Bronwen's lemon balm
Arrives at my door
Slightly wilted
In a plastic bag.
A present from Joanne
Who's moving,
Breaking up her garden.

I didn't notice it was growing
While Bronwen lay dying
Cancer boiling out her cheek
like angry red tar bubbles.

I blended smoothies washed glasses
Held my breath with the quiet
and order of the house
The perfect garden
Waiting for death

Which came
At summer's end
Spiders spinning webs
Bronwen gone

Her poems left unmothered.

It spreads like wildfire, Joanne says,
Contain it.

But to me
Bron's lemon balm
is living poetry
Let it fight and twine
with oregano and mint.
It took fourteen years
to get here –
Let it thrive.

GABRIELLE SANTYR

Mandala

I'm waiting for you under the clock – but I thought
You went by and did not stop...

This clock face has circled the centuries
ordering sequence and meaning,
into numbers without end
into chimes that rejoice and mourn;
watchful as a mandala over the hurried square.

In the traffic seconds count, cars dart in and out
merging from one revolution to the next:
repeating old mantras and mistakes.
Has he exited the roundabout – changed his mind?
Did he see disorder in my dress? A secret ugliness?

I lift my shoulders, firm my chin, gaze like a stalking hawk
over the dark cobbles of number and symbol
– nines running into zeros –
who can track these wheeling zillions?

I check again my watch...
clutch my wrist and secure
the band that cuffs me into place –

still wait a lover's wait beneath the ticking clock

The Verandah

a frail feather caught in a cobweb
on the balustrade
shivers in the wind
as I wait for you at day's end

wondering what mood you'll be in
what crankiness attached to those stale bagels
you bought –
about to be tossed
where wanderers may find them in their evening
diggings –
the shed poppy seeds along your route
a pittance for the hungry sparrow

dry yellowed broccoli
is better than none –
you really don't like it but like to save pennies:
banking on beans and barley
tuna in caseloads
the bitterness of soy

Elyse drains milk from me and
I save butter-smooth words for you

but our bedsprings are hard
and puncture my ribs
down duvets are remote and I need
that dark poppy juice now: for
the slope is as steep
and the house on the hill is unreal in
the grey light from town

Wild Raspberries

Why do I have to have everything
perfect?
The pillows smooth
the mattress just so
the bed all made as if to show
I never slept in it
or did anything so human in my life
as sleep
snore like you – never
flush toilets   dampen tissues   crumple towels
mash real food around my mouth
let tears run   have knots in my hair
be unsoaped for once
just washed by rain
in a feral wilderness

letting the earth smells in
bestirring up my sweat
pine cones stopping up my ears
eyelids rustling leaves
berry breasts resting on green moss
waiting for some horned animal
in velvet rut to seize me by the nape
press me into that earth that soil

Rasp licking   tongue berrying
staining all my closenesses
with juicy loosenesses
presented with a hunter's flourish
to his prey...

A corsage long buried
in a closed drawer and
berries that no longer taste or smell
are shriveled crimson black

but you – you are still there
in our perfect bed
remembering

wild wild raspberries

Serpentine

What is
the serpent? You may say:

a basket case
dancing to flutes
tempting Eve and Ulysses
with wicked undulations

speaking with silver forked tongue
and rattling its chain mail
before the lethal strike then
– forget the tourniquet –
loosely shedding guilty skins and
sliding through our dark unconsciousness.

After swallowing eggs whole
and regurgitating rosy apples
– missing out on words of wisdom
or indicators of direction –
it is choking us with its torque
of figure eight configurations
in merely molecular formation

but end to end – a coil
and we are collared
in this asylum that we call home
this double-walled helix
of our discontent.

PATIENCE WHEATLEY

The Birth of Venus

Sandro Botticelli 1444-1510

A shell releases her
As Zephyrs gently blow

With bellows cheeks
and crinkled amniotic ripples

lap her scalloped craft
and Spring in gauzy flowered gown

delivers her with long wavy tresses
modestly disposed

But she's not really
Goddess – she's Renaissance

A second birth of classical beauty
Carrying genes of marble Venuses

Lost now under rubble
And dry monks' plainsong

Yet rising once again
With birds and flowers and perfumed airs

In this our shattered
new millennium.

A Subversive

like that other who
lurked in the
shadows of your childhood
stealing your mother's attention
with hidden laughter
now squatting on the desk
asking to be milked of
green poems

She's hunched before it
a machine
you can't fight
seems to get into bed with you
and all through the night you hear

squeaking as it deals in
words or worse
symbols
disappearing at a touch –
as it clicks digestively

chewing in its operating system
the cud of
revolution.

Kissing Under a Winter Sky

You expect nothing
and the surprise of it tips
you into the thought

Why was *this* so enjoyable?

like the mild shock sometimes
encountered at New Year's Eve parties
meaningless yet intriguing that
can fit you under the bow of Orion
shove you under the kilt of Perseus, and the square belly of his horse.

Cassiopeia weeps, Andromeda laughs.

And you think perhaps
you're young as they are

Summer Tennis

Throwing a green ball high
against the milk-blue
sky of early summer
you serve for the inner
corner of the court
expect a hard return

but throwing an old thought high
against the August glare
of a sun ringed for rain
you slap it
to the outer corners
and the thought hurtles back
spinning a new way
in an unexpected place

throwing a ball up far
into the indigo sky of late summer
you keep the rhythm of the volley
with deep breathing
free breathing
and concentrate on the good stroke
in the short life
of summer.

LAURIE LEWIS

New York Sweet

Ghost of Ira
Cold night standing in line at the Village Vanguard,
some guy from Indiana in front of us, grey frizzled hair,
and his friend who played with Mingus and
has a paid up mortgage.
The ghost of an old friend slides past,
black and homeless, layered clothes,
a tooth missing from his smile,
finessing a handout.
Stay sweet, he says.

Crazy MoMA
Outside, middle-aged matron at the hot dog vendor,
I hate ketchup, she says to her friend.
You're kidding, you hate it too? That's amazing.
I HATE ketchup.
In the shimmering museum, brain mashed,
eyes and mind go to
play among the artifacts.
A voice from behind the partition.
Body parts, she says, *I hate body parts.*
You too? That's amazing.
I HATE body parts.

East Village
Black clad, fashionable, with all the confidence money can buy,
   cellphones clapped to their heads like members of some
   deformed demented species born with a thumb in its ear.
Brown nannies in trench coats, smooth expressionless faces, cool
   in khaki, pushing strollers past secure doorways and upscale
   Italian restaurants. No room for racial angst, for political

unrest; working for good references and holiday entitlements,
their own kids in day care or with Sistah.
White babies, tiny, rosy-cheeked, dozing in carriages, swaddled in
fleecy pink, robin's egg blue, daffodil yellow, leaf green.
Irresistible spring comes to Manhattan.

Swimming close to the truth

At a swimming pool near the equator I am learning to swim at
last. A child hangs from a yellow rope, a water-bug, all knees
and elbows, moving herself along. Her small perfect face
confronts mine above the water.

You are very old, she says. *I noticed that this morning,* I tell her. She
is looking at my pale northern face, my thin hair dripping.

You are very old, she says. *If you think I'm old, you should see my
mother.* She watches my mouth move, the lines around my lips.

You are very old, she says. *It happens to everyone.* She sees my
naked eyelids blink over blue marbles.

You are very old, she says. *It's been a hard life.* She reads the
furrows and wrinkles of my life. I am running out of answers.

There is no defence against her small truth.

I think about holding her head under the blue water. The pure
sunny justice of it. No one will ever say it to *her* – *she* will never
be very old.

But I wave to the waiter and order a rum punch at poolside. It's
one of the privileges of age.

All my own work

As I come into class he yells at me, one of my fellow students:
"Is this all your own story?" he hollers.
I look at the first page. "Yes, it's my story."
"Is it all your own punctuation?" he shouts.

All mine? I'd never thought –
I'm not really sure –

That semi-colon;
I might have borrowed it from someone.
Maybe Elizabeth. She usually has lots on hand;
so I guess she doesn't need it back, not right away.

But the periods are mine.
They are easy. They're just little dots.
Sitting on the bottom line.
When you want to stop.

And I think I used only one apostrophe.
It's sort of like the finger of God,
that little curly thing, pointing down from the sky,
so that you've got to be very careful where you put it.
It's mine, all right.
God gave it to me.

I know for sure that the commas are all mine.
Because I make mine just like an apostrophe
only I sit it down at the bottom of the line,
with the little tail dangling down
like putting your big toe in the bathtub
to test the water,
when you need a bit of a rest.

Question mark?
Did I have one? Sure, right at the end of my story.
They are really useful and I keep a bunch
in the cookie jar, because they are like heart-shaped cookies
that break in half so each piece is like a person's ear.
Because when you say a question, that's where it has to go.
Right to someone's ear. Right?

But exclamation marks, well!
I haven't used an exclamation mark since I was a kid;
maybe I used up my whole lifetime's supply right then,
for all the things that were really exciting or noisy,
like things are when you're a kid.
Running, shouting, birthdays, presents!
Oh!
But if I really needed one now, I could probably rent it for a bit.
They make such a racket if you leave them lying around the house.

But I guess I can't tell him all that,
so I just say,
"Right, it's all mine. Every bit of it."

REBECCA LUCE-KAPLER

Kate's Edna

Foggy night in autumn. Deep within,
a southern heat and sharp corset.
I watch her white body spill
from the confines of dress, the flash of lightning.
Her hair falls about her shoulders,
shaken loose from the pins. I lift
my own thickness from my neck, loving
the rounded curves of her body
sliding into the waves of the gulf,
her arms outstretched.
She is naked moonlight
polished by late-rising stars,
a wraith upon the water.
She dissolves with every step,
her fingertips, then her arms, smaller
than clam shells across the sand.
Soon she will slip beneath the surface
a trail of bubbles marking
the last of her sighs
that expect no answer.
Only the brush of her breath
will touch cheeks
of young women longing
to sing on their own.

Growing Up with Women

She barely remembers
November of the sudden crash,
the car of her father's train tumbling
from a collapsing bridge, bodies scattered
everywhere into the Missouri river.

She lives in a house filled with scent
of lavender sachet that leaks from drawers
and mingles with starch from petticoats
ironed on Tuesday.

No stiff white shirts and black ties
crowd the backyard clothesline.
Woolen pants draped over chairs
are given to household slaves.

She speaks her mind at supper
asks great-grandmère for the latest gossip
a fascination for women entangled
in desire and duty. The soft French voice
slips across the tablecloth,
cool fire like fields of poppies at night.

Without men to guide the conversation
women encourage her to have opinions,
bright motes of morning light. All during that spring
she remembers what the nuns taught her
about literature and music. How one
can find corridors in mathematics
numbers slipping off her tongue like sweet cherries.
She revels in their important attention.

And at night, she and Kitty read Dickens with candles,
their shadows splashed across the porch swing.
They sip the words, speaking them aloud to one another,
colouring their lips. Their skin
ripples in the dim light, every paragraph
a different detail played across the house.
When they tire of reading,
their eyelids fluttering with stars,
they hold hands and whisper dark
stories that cast visions before them
on whitewashed walls. Kitty's voice
warm in her ear as she shares a secret.

       That year,
she learns the intimacy of women,
a smooth wind sliding through windows
from mimosa to her fingers, brightening
quiet moments, their voices
laughing in every corner.

With Maupassant

beneath the hard whale
bone of her corset
french memory flushed
her skin, urged her
to sear maupassant's words
onto american pages

late night in sticky st. louis summers
his words slid
up her flesh escaping
constraint
spilling her body
from wooden chairs
as she wrote herself
across the persian carpet
pages fluttering
from her fingers
to whitegloved editors
who shrieked at the orchids
  their flanks, odorant, and transparent,
  open for love and more tempting than all women's flesh
denying them the printing
press

JILL BATTSON

Why you should be jailed, Martha

Not because you got greedy, or embezzled money
not because I am jealous of your business acumen
or that you never seem to age
but because you make me dissatisfied with my life
every month when my Martha Stewart Living arrives in the mailbox
I compare my life to chocolate box fantasies
thumb the pages past Santa Fe cookout brunches
tips on how to wash your pet dog, hang the perfect family portrait
or give a simple, but knock-out, party on your Catskills dock
every month my heart wrenches its beat into longing
I want a whitewashed plank dock with wicker chairs to bask in at sunset
I want to be able to wash my dog with an expensive natural sponge
– and then throw it away
I want a family to cook for – a family, damn it!
why didn't I think of turning boring cheap pillow ticking
into myriad coloured dyed napkins with fringes?
why is my evening meal – an evening meal
rather than a cornucopia of colours, textures
and the right balance of food groups served in a white porcelain bowl?
Martha, you make me need things I never imagined I wanted
a scrubbed pine, french baroque inspired kitchen table
with just the right hint of spearmint green/white paint glaze
magic floating candles made from muffin tin molds
six ways to prepare bruschetta including fava bean with arugula pesto
and apple cheeked blonde children and a husband to cook for
I never imagined I needed a husband
Martha, my paycheque won't support a second home in Kentucky blue
                                        grass country
my friends barely visit me in Ontario, let alone spend weeks
lounging on a ivy covered porch watching me collect jelly glasses
or invent new ways to serve unusual appetizers made from kalamata
                                        olives and mayonnaise
Martha, I blame you for my newly acquired over-spending habit
to prepare simple grilled chicken and a fatoush salad

I need to buy a thousand dollar Weber barbecue, new plates from
                                        Williams Sonoma
and balsamic vinegar that costs more than any good bottle of wine
                                        I'll ever drink
Martha, I do not have hours to spend sniffing for the perfect
                                        cantaloupe in farmers' markets
or piercing corn kernels with my fingernail to see if they leak white
                                        fluid that proves they're ripe
my days are not spent dreaming of ways to display colour
                                        coordinated wildflowers in large seashells
or wondering how the american flag should be displayed and if it
                                        should come in at night
I would need a husband to manage that
but I don't have one
and I don't have an large, extended, perfectly behaved, photogenic,
                                        toothsome family with shiny hair
to sit around on my overstuffed chintz (covered by me) sofa
or children running around the house giggling with their
                                        renovated antique toys found at flea markets
and Martha, while I don't blame you for your lapse in judgement
when you thought you didn't have as many millions as a self-made
                                        business woman should
I do blame you for my discontent
and you should be jailed, Martha, for publishing that magazine
that glossy, full colour, pornographic catalogue of consumerism
                                        you call
Martha Stewart Living
and I blame you, Martha, that I can't tear myself away from it each
                                        and every month.

In Irving Layton's Greece

I find it strange that colour photographs from the 70s
always seem to lose their reds and blues   – *L. Cohen*

Dorothy is the kind of woman who dresses for the journey
the kind of woman who dresses for situation or location

we know this from flipping through the towering pile
of four-year-dust-covered photograph albums in Dorothy's apartment

Dorothy is in a Greek market wearing a yellow and white striped caftan
to the floor it sweeps gold-coined sandals and red toenails

the photo has lost its other primary colours giving everything
a haze of sand, sun, a mediterranean glow, the yellow of change

Dorothy's hair is long, wavy, honey blonde pulled back with a band –
Deneuve-like
makes her more attractive than she's ever been

Irving Layton, a bombastic whirlwind of poetry, while teaching at York
told a story of a witch he met in Greece who foretold the end of the world

Dorothy is drinking a beige martini under a bower of grape leaves
her long tapered fingers offer up condensated glass to photographer

the caftan makes its appearance on patios, ships' decks, narrow streets
against ancient sandstone walls punctuated by dull orange metal rings

Dorothy and the caftan are reclining on a wall that overlooks the dark night
they are back to back with Dorothy's husband, the painter RB

RB said that Irving was an impossible monster who thrilled the students
but needed taking down a peg or two, and RB did

Dorothy wears her impressive grin across sandy skin
the caftan drapes mid-stride suggestion beautifully around her hips and
                                                                    legs

the photographs suggest no other changes of clothing on the three month
                                                                    trip
RB said it was magical, beautiful and a very bad time.

CAROLYN SMART

October

Those fallen leaves, pale supplicants,
have much to teach us of surrender,
how, wrapped in autumn's incense
they unfurl their flags to the wind

Every year I want to kneel in damp soil
and say farewell to blessed things:
the swift geese as they shout each to each
above the treetops, the white nicotinia
at my door, still releasing its fragrance
against the chill of evening,
the memory of a much-loved hand
the last day I held it

There was early morning light rich as silk,
the flash of late fireflies
amidst the cedar,
cows' tails whisking in the amber fields,
the chiaroscuro of a moth's wing

Goodbye, brief lives,
ablaze with tenderness;
today the glory of the leaves
is enough, for I am learning anew
to release all I cannot hold,
these moments of luminous grace
saying Here and here is beauty,
here grief: this is the way to come home

Walking to the Ocean: Dawn

I am too tired for sentimentality,
and the ocean looks cold, so
I press your cheek to mine, Daniel,
and we walk out along the promenade –
you held high in my arms

It seems natural to be lost in the roll of waves
and the sawing of insects,
all night to lie hearing this,
then stand up and walk to the ocean
while the heat grows around us
like a room filling up with parachutes

Hold my hand now, Daniel,
your plum-size fist
and darkening lashes precise as flames
When the doctor cut me open
and saw you crouching there
my tenderness spilled out
Grey, wet boy they pummelled into life,
what do words like need or sorrow
mean to you, full or less, my care
for you all in this outstretched hand

We walk to the empty beach,
I am thinking cleanly of your birth
How could I have imagined
a love as artless as this

Wolf Swamp Road

The boys in the back seat rattle on,
toughing each other, drenched in the cologne
that tells its own treacherous tale,
their eyes like saucers, moons,
as dark and cold as the climate they were born to

When they were little
they would hold their lips just so,
run with capes, fight shadows with their swords,
now sleepless and eager for the fury of years ahead,
angrily they stare at their mutable faces
in the bathroom mirror: a look,
it seems to them, devoid of any charm or talent,
they could bellow for the weight of their own dreams

We drive the stretch of thickest bush where
trees hang heavy after weeks of drought,
the boys in the back trying to be polite
or even just to tolerate an adult
while my son drives on into dusk

Up ahead a trick of the eye or not,
a tentative step onto tarmac:
one trembling brown-eyed spotted fawn

From the backseat in a newly broken voice:
if you'd gone a little faster
we'd've had 'em
it quivers into alien brush
and further, to the green and tangled night

DIANE DAWBER

Squares and Rounds: Pegs and Holes

Back when a penis was required
equipment for creative work
I didn't have one.

Back when a uterus was required
equipment for creative work
I no longer had one of those either.

When drinking and smoking
were required activities
for creative camaraderie
Both made me sick.

When business meetings were required
for creative camaraderie
I was too tired of meetings to arrange any.

If you want to talk poetry
you'll have to come for a walk
and drink water.

Cheque Paid

Through the hotel restaurant window
I see the gulls
arrive en masse in the low field
for breakfast.

In the hotel restaurant window
I see the guests
arrive en masse at their tables
for breakfast

Myself,
I am suspended
somewhere between the panes
not needing to go anywhere
fed
and paid in full.

Getting Where I'm Going

On the road out of Thunder Bay
I pass
over the great northern divide.
From here all rivers run to the Arctic Ocean
maybe taking the land with them
to the everlasting daylight
to the everlasting dark.

On the road to Upsala
I pass
into Central Time
contemplating whether road hum is inside me or out
internal chatter superimposed on
trees bearing witness along the margins
trees moving
felled and lashed to trucks.

When I stop for supper in Kenora
a bald eagle
cruises past the window
leaving a wide,
     open
          blue
              quiet
                   behind.

Educational Poster

All the visiting writers want one
so I look at the staff-room poster carefully
to see if it's just novelty to urban dwellers.

If you find a bear in your playground
it says
throw any food-containing items
toward the animal and away from yourself.
Retreat slowly facing it.
Do not turn away.
Do not run.
Go indoors.
Tell an adult.

I think there is more going on here,
after our quarrel this morning,
and I would add
if you are a bear in your playground
just hibernate until spring.

Fishing Camp Trophy

I should have noticed
her opaque expression
as her delicate hand hesitated over the room keys.

I assumed that all the rooms
smelled like very old ash trays
and had window gaps
the chill May air
invaded at will.

At supper in the diner
the self-proclaimed Vietnam vet
hogged the conversation
while she put away groceries
with lowered eyes.

The camp owner
drop-out executive from Toronto
cooked breakfast
and asked my satisfaction.

"What room were you in?"
he inquired and when I told him
he stopped
spatula in the air
with a considering look.

I guess she had her hooks set
and if she couldn't
dispatch the lunker –
the oversize pike engulfing her –
then I was a good enough proxy.

KRYSTLE MULLIN

This is not a poem

a brilliant or not so smart woman once wrote
if you don't expect anything from somebody you won't be
    disappointed
that woman put her head in the oven
and I am driving home
a much less tragic ending
but not on the highway
because the car won't go over 60
luxury automobile – not quite
The expectations I have of you are unsteered
the seat belt is copping a feel and I am unsure whether it is because
    my shirt is too short or if it is because I am a slut

speaking of which
another woman left my house early this morning upset
this was a kink in the linen to say the least
usually she is the one folded in the closet
while I am lying on the laundry room floor
I got home to discover you received the mail I sent
it remained unopened and unobserved
I wonder if it is you who doesn't get it or me.

if it is me my efforts are leveled out as a stupid silly old stubborn
    man who believes what witches tell him and whose partner
    can't learn the duties of a housewife if her life depended on it
    (and it did)
if it is you I am the heroic mold, a saintly stallion of a young man
    who kills and kills himself over and over for someone who is
    pretending she is dead or 'emotionally unavailable' as the kids
    are calling it these days

this is not a poem
this is whatever you want to call me waiting for you to arrive,
to hear you say
there has been a mix up
you didn't get the mail
and consequently you aren't Richard the third
or any such brute who has the power to ignore penmanship or the
    taste of an envelope

a brilliant or not so smart woman
once wrote
no matter how much you knelt and prayed, you still had to eat 3
    meals a day and have a job and live in the world
I suppose I can't make you open your mail or love me or read
    renaissance drama
but somehow I have found the faith
to believe that it is possible to
drive 60 on the highway
in a car that is maybe not so cool
and to escape
the bell jar

A Small Town Near Verona Ontario

Larry didn't want to have children because there are a number of albinos
  and dwarfs that run through his relations
his genetic pool is not a place for doing laps, and that makes him angry
his genes are jumping off the diving board doing cannon balls, so Larry
  decided to pull the plug
he up and got his tubes tied
needless to say Martha was pissed
Why'd you ask me to get married for if you didn't want to have children?
He thinks that she should be happy because she is liberated and doesn't
  have to participate in some control cycle where he is the boss of her
  because he is the man. And if they had children she would never be
  able to leave the house and would develop some problem that is so
  bad that they haven't even given it a name yet
She tells him that she doesn't give a hot flying fork full about some cycle
  of control – she wants children for Christ's sake
Larry tells her that she is being selfish and not even thinking about the
  feelings of their would-be children
For example, he says: there are no support group meetings held for
  albino dwarfs (not even in the city)
Martha didn't have time to deal with this because she had to go to work

Lucinda was upset because she was looking forward to being a
  bridesmaid
(she was eating the strawberry rhubarb special at Milton's Piehole)
she had planned the whole thing out
she would be rolling down the aisle in her beautiful marigold dress
her hair would be swept up (like the woman who sells the perfect flip
  frying pan on the home shopping network has hers done)
she would approach the alter when, suddenly, she would see him
the most handsomest man she could ever dream of
(not like the fellas here who have no respect)
they would make eye contact and he would smile
then they would live happily ever after
somewhere miles away from town
(maybe even in the city)
where they have ramps and bigger stalls in public bathrooms

Milton wondered why Mrs. Brown always came in looking for a chat

she never had anything new or exciting to say
and neither did he, for that matter
but still, day in and day out she came here to talk
(except on Sundays, of course)
he looked at the pie she was polishing off
no use in asking her if she'll want more
cause she will
he called out to Martha to cut another slice of cherry
she was a good enough girl, that Martha
always working hard but never really doing much of anything else
Milton had overheard Lucinda talking to herself
Martha had called off the wedding
all for the better, young people don't know what they are getting
    themselves into these days
he had married young and stayed married
though he never felt anything beyond a genuine comfort when he was
    around his wife
(who was dead now)
he didn't even think that love existed
how could it?
love was just something that people wanted so badly they start to
    believe in
he didn't even know if what he felt for his three sons was love
he knew that he could live without them
so how can you love someone if you don't need them?
ding ding
the cherry pie was up
he brought it over to Mrs. Brown and placed the full plate on top of
    the empty one
How the boys doing, Mil? she asked.
Fine, fine. They're just fine. He replied
Can't believe how you do it, she said while stabbing the crust with her
    fork
Three boys to look after – all going through the change. Must be hard
    on the nerves…well never mind – I see you've done a good
    enough job. That Larry though, he's a funny one ain't he? Hey,
    you got any water boiling? I'd love a cup of tea. Martha, don't
    put any honey in it this time – I just can't stand anything sweet.

NATHALIE SORENSEN

The Springs

Pressed hard against jagged craters and
sweeping lava flows of dead volcanoes
frozen to stone eons ago,
the bones of the Roman city lie exposed.
Low stone walls, delicate, orderly
delineate streets and squares, homes and shops.
Here and there fluted columns stand
as they did two thousand years ago
when this was Glanum, outpost of empire
in the wild western region of Gaul.

I stand on a ridge of cliffside, peering down
looking for something,
not stones, not fragments of carvings,
not broken figures from friezes of war.
I am looking for water.
For in this hot dry city, I have read,
there is a spring, an ancient spring
known to the indigenous people of this place.

I see them, the Ligurians, the old ones
before the Romans, before the Gauls,
before the Western Goths who sacked this city sixteen centuries ago.
They gather round their campfires in the gloom
telling of the hunt, sharpening arrows,
refining bits of wisdom in the night,
and pulling clear pure water from their spring.

Back down in the city
I search through the streets and alleys,
and come upon the spa of Valetudo
goddess of health-giving waters. There she is
carved in her niche, headless,
still presiding over her bath –

down well worn steps, a pool of
brackish water, festooned with algae,
holding the dregs of empire all these years.
Then I see them –
more steps, leading up, away
from Valetudo's spa, straight up the mountain.
High on a pinnacle, high over the city,
there is the cleft in the rock, the orifice I seek.

I clamber closer and peer down. All is dark and dry
no sound of water.
I listen, pitch my ear for echoes
beyond the dry grass, the volcanic rocks.
When did the sacred spring last gurgle through this well?
My whole being bent to attention, I wait
but everywhere, silence.
No faint murmur, whisper of flow,
no scent of wetness coming through.
All I hear is dry grass rustling
cicadas shrilling in the heat,
and I am comfortless as I depart.

Months later, I am swimming
in the river by my home
in the river I call home.
The mist is golden in the early sun
the undulant surface green, green and amethyst.
By the bank a white water lily,
gently rocked by ripples, opens its heart.

I drift in the tranquil current dreaming
and there they are, the ancient ones, gathered
here into me, smiling, complete.

As I calmly stroke, water washes through my mouth, soft and clean.

Zen Garden at Kokedera

In the year 1339, in the city of Kyoto
Muso Soseki built a waterfall
without a drop of water,
a dry cataract of boulders
tumbling immobile down the hill
these six centuries and more.
Approach with care.
Here the silence roars.

Everywhere else, moss, moist and fresh
a hundred kinds, mauve, brown,
orange, grey, shade upon shade of green
envelops the rocks, spreading gently, calmly,
to the pond below, pure land garden of paradise.
All around it, a path, following curves,
leads through the trees to the water
and up again, yes, up again
for the dry cascade
stripped to the bare bones
is calling, shouting
wake up! wake up!

The Holiness of Plants

On the island of Shikoku, near a small Shinto shrine
towers an immense pine tree. Worshippers circle its trunk
with a ring of thick rope; this is sacred ground.

In Thailand Buddhist monks conduct
tree ordinations, wrapping orange
robes around the boles. Ritually blessed water
is passed around, and foresters spare
these arboreal clergy from the axe.

In tenth century Japan, priests and monks
debate the question
"Can trees and plants be enlightened?"
Yes, says Ryogen, Abbott of Mount Hiei, who
sees the shrubs and flowers in his garden
as yogis in meditation, sitting
silent, still, on their way to nirvana.

This morning I, too, sit in my garden,
hands folded, head bowed.
Around me nasturtiums
glow orange under leaf umbrellas.
Rose azaleas flicker scarlet
against purple aster, deep blue monkshood.
The early sun, without distinction,
burnishes us all.
Drenched in light, we glimmer and glisten
enlightened, enveloped, so tenderly
held in the mystery.

MARY CAMERON

Tranquillizer

Somewhere a stream ripples in the dark,
leaves move against the moon and stars

and owls and night-
moving animals make small

perfect decisions without
thinking.

Deucalion and Pyrrha

I hate to turn this back to love,
but if there were another great flood
and you were left rowing your wife
over fields and factories, the brief
spattering of rain's last aftershock
affecting you both and you stopped,
finally, to worship, roping your craft
to spires of the *NY Times* (fore and aft)
I hope she'd read the oracle to mean
throw rocks to build women and men,
not strike us down, rubble and bone;
but change our hatred into stone.
*No better man than this, no one more fond
of right*, unyielding, rough and sullen,
you'd begin with her our future round
with the gods you've found, distrusting heaven.

All Clothing is Terrible

First the fig leaf, then the leaved
corsets and gowns, fluttering many folds,

reeds over stones, draining streams.
Close up, the layering above,

below the skin. Soon stripped, soon
back to branch-thin, we believe

that covers make smooth thinking.
Who told you that you were naked?

What routes and bounty can be taken
by the disciplined skin?

Sons of Blood

Was that you I saw in *Time*
with the placard and fist, line
indecipherable so probably obscene,
spurning the Coeur d'Alene
boys, their swastikas and uniforms beneath
mouths of broken jeers, black teeth,
trashed entrances to tombs?
You vs. shaved thugs whose qualms
must be miniscule (they'd batter gravity
if they could), bridled, military
or worse, absolving nothing but hatred.
You with your sprung, wrecked beard
and the good fight, resisting cruelty,
and just this photograph disputing your obscurity?

JASON HEROUX

Story

One summer night a stranger
threw an artificial leg onto my lawn

made of plastic, leather, steel.
The garbagemen left it there.

Sunday, my neighbour put on
a yard sale. He rang my bell

and swore, "Christ, you got to get
rid of that thing because people

think I'm trying to sell it. I'm
losing business." All our yards

are jammed together – my other
neighbour grows a garden in hers

and throws a tattered trenchcoat
and fedora over the For Sale sign

in my yard, to frighten off birds.
I haven't received mail in weeks.

Last night, I carried the leg to
the lake and threw it into the dark

blue sheets of water where it thrashed
as if waking from a terrible dream.

Dark Jars

There is a place
where doctors
remove people's shadows
from their bodies for free.

A friend of mine went there.

I never saw him again.

But he told me about it
last night in a dream.

"The shadows are kept
in jars," he said.

"The jars are so dark.
They all look the same.
And no one knows whose
is whose."

The Spoon

He picked up the spoon.
"What are you doing?" the spoon asked.
"I'm about to eat lunch," he said.

"But I'll drown if you put me into the soup."
"You won't drown," he said. "You're a spoon."
"I'll drown," the spoon said.

He put the spoon in the soup and held it there for a long time.
The handle twitched. Little bubbles appeared on the surface of the
soup. He was afraid to lift the spoon up, afraid to put it inside his
mouth.
The soup grew colder and colder.

Evening Postscript

The taxi rumbles
    in the empty street
Like a straw at the bottom
    of a glass.
A moment later
    everything is quiet:

the dead have called
    us here to make
an important announcement,
    and all
the grass leans
    in one direction like
microphones during
    a press conference.

The stores are closed,
    but the earth is open.
Our shadows pass through
    the grassy turnstiles,

and the spider in her web
    wakes up twitching
like a small dark glove
    when the hand enters.

STEVEN HEIGHTON

Address Book

Bad luck, it's said, to enter your own name
and numbers in the new address book.
All the same, as you slowly comb
through the old one for things to pick

out and transfer, you are tempted to coin
yourself a sparkling new address,
new name, befitting the freshness of this clean-
slating, this brisk kiss

so long to the heart-renders – every friend
you buried or let drift, those Home for the Aged
maiden relations, who never raged
against the dying of anything, and in the end

just died. An end to the casualties pressed
randomly between pages – smudged, scribbled chits
with lost names, business cards with their faded
bold-fronts of confidence, solvency. The palimpsest

time made of each page; the hypocrite it made
of you. Annie, whom you tried two years to love
because she was straight-hearted, lively, and in love
with you (but no strong-arming your cells and blood);

Mad Carl, who typed poet-to-poet squibs in the pseudo-
hickish, hectoring style of Pound, all sermonfire
and block caps, as AINT FIBRE ENOUGH HERE, BOYO,
BACK TO THE OLE FLAX FIELD . . . this *re* a score

of your nature poems. When he finally vanished
into the far east, you didn't mind the silence.
Still, this guilt, as if it weighs in the balance,
every choice – as if each time your pen banished

a name it must be sensed somewhere, a ballpoint stab, hex-
needle to the heart, the treacherous
innocent *no* of Peter, every X
on the page a turncoat kiss. . . .

Bad luck, it's said, to enter your own name in the new
book – as if, years on, in the next culling,
an executor will be leafing through and calling
or sending word to every name but you.

Blackjack

Hit: to take another card, and risk breaking.
Stand: to stick with what you have.

The dealer is dailiness, and the asking –
hit or stand? – comes more often than you guess.
Missed cues can fill a life. Or you signal wrong,

the house responds, no recourse. Standing with less
may be safer – you know the odds – but even then
the temptation is to hit. Sometimes loss

at long odds looks better than a sure win;
as if winning were a sure thing, ever.
In some dreams a familiar house will open

into unsuspected rooms, door after door
glides ajar, yet you hang back and consciousness
cuts in like an eviction. But what if you were

not so anxious to wake back into your less
uncharted life, and chanced those farther rooms . . .?
Caution cancels love's richer part; eros,

sequestered in home safety, always seems
to die by inches. The house wins by turning
its people into furniture. Many tombs

are made of unplayed cards. It's me I'm warning
here. Hit when the asking happens. The house
may have its system, but you're not through learning.

The Wood of Halfway Through

A daughter

Any forest craves torrents
of breeze in noon's steeper blaze: as a glider
seeks thermals coiled into high currents,
each aerial a ladder

into middle air. Appearance
never speaks for marrow. I think I was sadder
before you than friends saw. Now all my *aren'ts*
and *shouldn'ts* recede, I'm the reader

of a tongue lacking the negative mood,
the conditional, and other places to hide.
Who is it loves you, his heart now a lantern

in the dark wood of halfway through? The one
you made solid when he felt himself shade,
who made his way back from the border, made good.

ABOUT THE POETS

ACKNOWLEDGEMENTS

A BOUT THE POETS

JILL BATTSON is an internationally published poet and poetry activist. She has been widely featured in literary journals and anthologies in North America and the U.K. and has performed her work around the globe. Her first book *Hard Candy* was nominated for the Gerald Lampert Award. Jill's latest book of poems is *Ashes are Bone and Dust* (Insomniac Press).

MARY CAMERON's first book of poetry, *Clouds without heaven*, was nominated for the Gerald Lampert Award in 1998. She has been editor of *Quarry* magazine, and poetry editor of *Prism International*. Her poems have appeared in many Canadian journals and in the Banff Centre's anthology, *Meltwater*.

M. E. CSAMER has been widely published in Canadian literary magazines. Her first collection *Paper Moon* appeared in 1998. A former board member of The ArtBar poetry reading series in Toronto, she currently serves as President of the League of Canadian Poets. Her latest book is *Light is What We Live In* (Artful Codger Press, 2005).

SANDRA DAVIES is a retired palliative care nurse who lives on Whitefish Lake in the woods north of Kingston with her partner Peter, her cat Spencer, and her golden retriever Lil. This is her first published work.

DIANE DAWBER, author of seven published books, is anthologized in Canada, the U.S.A. and the U.K., in texts for both adults and younger readers. Her next volume, *Looking for Snow Fleas*, is in the works at Borealis Press.

ERIN FOLEY: born and raised in Kingston, she is a recent graduate of Queen's University and currently enrolled in the Humber School for Writers. Erin's poems have appeared in *Lake Effect 2*, Queen's *Undergraduate Review* and *Ultraviolet*. Erin is honoured to be a part of this collection and this community.

ERIC FOLSOM was born in New England and has lived in Montreal, in Halifax, and for thirty years in Kingston, Ontario. He is the author of several collections of poetry, most recently *Northeastern Anti-Ghazals* (above/ground press) and *Icon Driven* (Wolsak and Wynn).

HOLLAY GHADERY came to Kingston in 2000 to study English Literature at Queen's University. Since graduating in 2004, she has attended the Summer Writing Experience at Sage Hill, published some poems while developing a fondness for Indian food and non sequiturs. Hollay also harbours an inordinate predilection for odd numbers, claiming they're not as pretentious.

ELIZABETH GREENE edited *We Who Can Fly: Poems, Essays and Memories in Honour of Adele Wiseman* (Cormorant, 1997) and co-edited two other collections of previously unpublished Canadian prose and poetry. She began to write poetry after "hearing" Sylvia Plath ranting at Ted Hughes on his arrival in the afterlife, October 28, 1998. She teaches Contemporary Canadian Women Writers at Queen's.

STEVEN HEIGHTON has published four books of poetry, most recently *The Address Book* (Anansi, 2004), and four books of fiction, most recently a novel, *Afterlands*, (Knopf Canada, 2005) which will also appear in the U.S., Britain, Australia, Germany and Holland. He is currently working on new poems and translations.

JASON HEROUX's poetry has appeared in literary journals in Canada, the U.S., Belgium, England, Ireland, and India, and was selected for *Breathing Fire 2: Canada's New Poets* (Nightwood Editions, 2004). His debut collection of poems, *Memoirs Of An Alias*, was published by The Mansfield Press in 2004.

HELEN HUMPHREYS has written four books of poetry and four novels. Her latest novel is *Wild Dogs*.

TARA KAINER was a member of Foxglove Collective, editors of the anthology, *On the Threshold: Writing Toward the Year 2000* (Beach Holme, 1999), and a co-organizer of the literary reading series, Kargo Cultur. An anti-poverty activist, she works and lives in Kingston.

PAUL KELLEY'S poem cycle "Only undo" appeared last year in the anthology *Companions and Horizons* (Vancouver: West Coast Line Press, 2005), and a selection of eleven poems from his *Learning the Light* appears in *W 11* [Elf], the journal of the Kootenay School of Writing.

LAURIE LEWIS is a Fellow of the Graphic Designers of Canada and is editor and art director of *Vista*, the magazine of the Seniors Association. Her work has been on CBC and CFRC and has been published in *Contemporary Verse 2, Queen's Feminist Review,* and the *Ottawa Citizen.* Laurie's publishing company, Artful Codger Press, specializes in the work of Kingston writers.

MARIE LLOYD has been writing poetry fitfully since childhood. Her favourite poets are Charles Simic and Wislawa Szymborska.

REBECCA LUCE-KAPLER is an associate professor of language and literacy in the Faculty of Education, Queen's University. She is the author of *The Gardens Where She Dreams*, a collection of poetry, and *Writing With, Through and Beyond the Text: An Ecology of Language.*

GABRIELLE MCINTIRE teaches literature at Queen's University in Kingston, and has published poetry in Canada, the United States, and England. She is at work completing a novel. She dedicates these poems to her mother, MCKMS.

KRYSTLE MULLIN has a B.A.H. and a Master's degree in Literature from Queen's University. She is currently applying to do her PhD in Creative Writing and working on a novel. A sele ction from her novel is going to be included in the forthcoming collection of short stories entitled *Sojourners: Narratives by Canadian Women.*

Louise O'Donnell has had poems published across Canada, in the U.S. and in Australia. In 2003 she collaborated with photographer Wayne McNulty to produce *Infinite Horizons*, poems in response to McNulty's photographs. She published *Shuffling Into Place* in March 2005. In July, a play based on this book was performed at Milford Playhouse.

Joanne Page is a Kingston writer and visual artist with two collections of poetry: *The River &The Lake* and *Persuasion for a Mathematician*. She is currently working on "The Future Will be Written in Water," a project embracing text, image and music.

Gabrielle Santyr's first collection of poetry, *Beastly Metaphors*, was published in 2005 (Artful Codger Press). She is a retired teacher, has taught creative writing, written magazine and newspaper articles, and edited a professional teachers' publication. She lives in Kingston.

Carolyn Smart moved to the Kingston area in 1983 after a very good blind date. She now lives (with the same date) on the edge of the Canadian Shield, cultivating hemerocallis. In the non-gardening months, she writes poems and memoir, and teaches Creative Writing at Queen's.

Nathalie Sorensen is retired from 26 years of teaching English at St. Lawrence College and doing graduate work in English literature and education. She enjoys reading, gardening, nature photography, and working for environmental preservation. She likes to spend time with her family at their woodlot and weekend house on the Salmon River.

Patience Wheatley grew up in England, became a Montrealer at the age of fifteen, and has lived in Kingston for about twenty years. She has had two books of poetry published by Goose Lane Editions, one by Pendas Productions, and recently a collection of short stories, *Camera Lucida* (Artful Codger Press 2006).

Acknowledgements

The editor and poets acknowledge with thanks the journals and books in which some of these poems were previously published.

M. E. Csamer: "Dying looked at me today" appeared in *Harpweaver*; "Maureen" first appeared in *Arc*.

Sandra Davies: These poems are part of a sequence, "Poems for My Lost Mother."

Erin Foley: "The Thing that Endures" and "Fuck the Secretary of Defence" appeared in *Lake Effect 2* (Artful Codger Press, 2005).

Eric Folsom: These poems were published in the 2005 chapbook *Northeastern Anti-Ghazals* from rob mclennan's above/ground press. An earlier version of "The Gore" appeared in *Poetry Halifax-Dartmouth*; an earlier version of "Slipping Away" appeared in *Lynx*.

Hollay Ghadery: "Tongue Rising" was first published in *Black Heart*.

Elizabeth Greene: "The Haunted Walk" first appeared in *The Kingston Eye Opener*; an earlier version of "Bronwen's Lemon Balm" appeared in *Queen's Feminist Review*.

Steven Heighton: These poems were previously published in *The Address Book* (Anansi, 2004).

Jason Heroux: These poems were previously published in *Memoirs of an Alias* (Mansfield Press, 2004).

Helen Humpheys: "Hurricane" first appeared in *Queen's Feminist Review*; "Foxes" was published in *Anthem* (Brick Books, 1999).

Tara Kainer: "Late Bloomer" and "It's the laughter" first appeared in *Queen's Feminist Review*.

LAURIE LEWIS: "New York Sweet" and "Swimming Close to the Truth" first appeared in *Queen's Feminist Review.*

REBECCA LUCE-KAPLER: "Kate's Edna" appeared in the *Journal of Curriculum Theorizing*, 16, Winter 2000 and in *Other Voices, 13* (2): 26-27. "Growing Up with Women" appeared in *Queen's Feminist Review*, 2004 and *Journal of Curriculum Theorizing, 16,* Winter 2000. "With Maupassant" appeared in *Queen's Feminist Review*, 2004 and *Journal of Curriculum Theorizing, 16,* Winter 2000.

GABRIELLE MCINTIRE: "Break Through" is forthcoming in *Small Brushes* (New Jersey).

LOUISE O'DONNELL: "Titania's Jewelry" first appeared in *Infinite Horizons*, (Strathcona Images, 2003).

GABRIELLE SANTYR: These poems first appeared in *Beastly Metaphors* (Artful Codger Press, 2005).

CAROLYN SMART: "October" and "Walking to the Ocean: Dawn" first appeared in *The Way to Come Home* (Brick Books, 1992).

PATIENCE WHEATLEY: "The Birth of Venus" first appeared in *The Astrologer's Daughter*, (Pendas Productions, 2004) and "Kissing Under a Winter Sky" in *Canadian Women Studies*, Vol 21 No 3, Winter 2002. "Summer Tennis" first appeared in the Newsletter of the Kingston Public Library and in *Queen's Quarterly* Vol 93 No 4, Winter 1986. "A Subversive" first appeared in Canadian Woman Studies Vol 11 No 2, Summer 1990. All four poems were included in the collection *The Astrologer's Daughter*, Pendas Productions, 2004.

The typeface used
in this book is
Minion, with Minion Swash Italic
and Minion Ornaments
The book was prepared for
publication by Laurie Lewis
at the
Artful Codger Press
Kingston, Ontario
2006